IMAGES
of America

DUBUQUE

THE 19TH CENTURY

Over three hundred trees were planted in Jackson Park in downtown Dubuque, between 6th and 7th Streets and Bluff and Locust Streets.

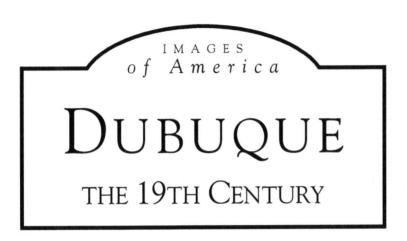

IMAGES
of America

DUBUQUE

THE 19TH CENTURY

John T. Tigges and James L. Shaffer

ARCADIA
PUBLISHING

Published by Arcadia Publishing
Charleston, South Carolina

Library of Congress Catalog Card Number: 00104921

For all general information contact Arcadia Publishing at:
Telephone 843-853-2070
Fax 843-853-0044
E-mail sales@arcadiapublishing.com
For customer service and orders:
Toll-Free 1-888-313-2665

Visit us on the Internet at www.arcadiapublishing.com

Dubuque's Main Street is shown here looking north in the late 1860s.

CONTENTS

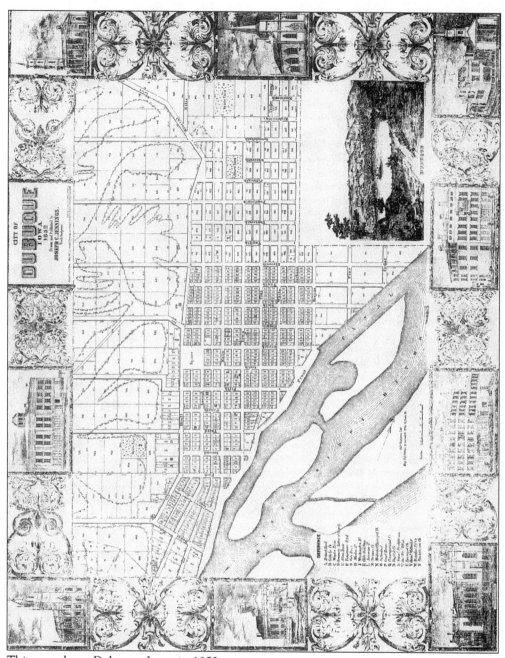

This map shows Dubuque, Iowa, in 1852.

INTRODUCTION

Dubuque, Iowa, situated on the west bank of the Mississippi River, is the oldest city in Iowa and lays claim to many unique features. For example, it is the home of the oldest college in Iowa (Loras College), which is also the second oldest college west of the Mississippi.

The area was explored and mined by two, if not three, men prior to Julien Dubuque's convincing argument to the Mesquakie Indians to permit him to work lead mines south of present-day city limits. Because he had opened the area and was successful in working with the Mesquakie, the city was named for him by those who later founded Dubuque in the 1830s. After Julien Dubuque died in 1810, the Mesquakie closed off the area to white settlers. It was not until June 1, 1833, that settlers moved in permanently under the settlement terms of the Blackhawk War. The tiny settlement soon swelled into a thriving river town. The original corporate limits, which included one square mile, were extended again in 1852.

The first settlers were attracted to the area because of lead ore. Mining was the major industry for a number of years, and shipments of hundreds of tons of lead "pigs" were floated annually by raft to St. Louis (location of the oldest college west of the Mississippi). However, the rich and fertile prairie lands soon brought an influx of settlers. The development of farms brought agriculture to the fore, and the city took its place in the pattern of Midwestern life. Dubuque soon became an important shipping point for farm commodities, as well as for those of the industrial centers of the territory.

The rapidly growing population of the city and the development of farms created a heavy demand for lumber. While a comparatively small percentage of the native timber was suitable for building (other than for log cabins), lumber mills were established, and at one time 15 such mills operated in and around Dubuque. Raft boats destined for Dubuque and its sawmills brought huge tows of pine logs from the Wisconsin and Minnesota forests, where such lumber was stored for shipment. For many years, Dubuque was one of the largest distributing points of lumber in the Midwest, and this attracted woodworking plants of every type. Timber remained the backbone of industry in the Key City for many years.

The first printing press in the Northwest Territory was erected in Dubuque, and in 1836, the *DuBuque Visitor* was published. It was the first newspaper in Iowa, and one of the first west of the Mississippi.

Railroads came to Dubuque from the east in 1855 when the Illinois Central Railroad came to Dunleith, Illinois, directly opposite Dubuque. In time, Andrew Carnegie sold that railroad an iron bridge to span the Mississippi River, and locomotives pulling their trains of freight into and out of Dubuque, along with their passenger trains, inspired Dubuquers to think of building their own railroads. North to Minnesota, south to Bellevue and Clinton, Iowa, westward to Farley, and beyond. The rails snaked their way across the Hawkeye State.

One banker, J.K. Graves, did not like the 30 minute ride to his place of business downtown from his home atop one of Dubuque's many bluffs. In time, he masterminded the Fenelon Place Elevator (or Fourth Street Cable Railway), which today is the shortest (296 feet) and steepest (a 63 percent grade) railway in the world. Once built, Graves could be at his office in less than five minutes, and was able to travel home in a similar amount of time.

The city's telephone history began in 1878, when the Dubuque Lumber Company installed two telephones, connecting its mill with the company's offices. The following year, the first central office was established, and served 12 telephones. A copy of the 1880 telephone directory is included in this volume.

Dubuque has many times been referred to as the "State of Dubuque," often bucking state-wide trends and preferring its own counsel. During the 19th century, Dubuque laid claim to the fact that the Speaker of the House of Representatives, David Henderson, was a Dubuquer but not a native born American. Because of his foreign birth, that was the highest office for which Henderson was eligible. Concurrently, Dubuquer William Boyd Allison, an Iowa Senator in Washington, chaired countless committees. He was offered the position of Secretary of Treasury twice: first in 1881, by President Garfield, and again in 1889, by President Benjamin Harrison. Near the end of the 19th century, President William McKinley offered Allison the office of Secretary of State. Again, he turned down the post. Both Henderson's and Allison's careers spanned an entire generation, each setting a then-current record for time in elected office. Henderson spent ten successive terms in the House, representing the Third Iowa District, while Allison served eight years as a Congressman and 35 years as a Senator, for a total of 43 years in public service. Not many towns or cities can lay claim to such political power.

Iowa, itself, was a political powerhouse. In addition to the two Dubuquers, Leslie Shaw of Denison, Iowa, was Secretary of the Treasury, and "Tama Jim" Wilson of Traer, Iowa, was Secretary of Agriculture during Henderson's time as Speaker.

While many of the scenes and buildings pictured in *Dubuque: The 19th Century* are gone, and remain only as photographic recollections, the memories that they conjure will give some insight into one of the most fascinating cities in the United States today.

ACKNOWLEDGMENTS

James L. Shaffer Collection
John T. Tigges Collection
Port of Dubuque Riverboat Museum
Center for Dubuque History, Loras College
Mary Starr, Telegraph Herald

Special thanks to Beth Mellentine, who donated several photos, and Kathryn E. Tigges, typist/proofreader.

One

1833–1873

This is an artist's impression of Julien Dubuque and his wife, Potosa. Early written descriptions of the couple resulted in what is probably a fairly accurate portrait.

After it was found covered with clapboard siding, this log cabin was moved from its location at 2nd and Locust Streets to Eagle Point Park, where it was restored. Years later, it was moved to a spot near the Ham House, a property of the Dubuque Historical Society. William Newman, a pioneer settler, occupied the cabin, although it was originally built by French hunters and miners. The year 1827 is sometimes mentioned, but it is, without a doubt, the oldest extant structure in the state of Iowa. This source information was obtained from the Langworthy documents, and statements from William Newman's nieces, Mrs. James J. Sullivan and Mrs. Norman Hurd of Dubuque.

The darker brick to the left was the original courthouse, while the lighter brick was an addition designed by John F. Rague, who also designed the Egyptian-style jail, which is to the left of the courthouse.

Here is the first map to show Iowa City as the capitol of Iowa territory. John Plumbe Jr., cartographer, finished it in 1839. Plumbe was a Dubuquer.

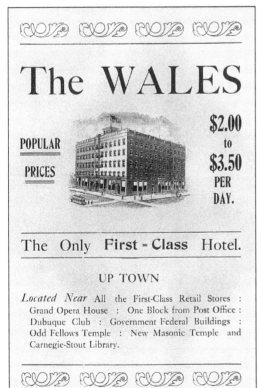

This is an advertisement for the Wales Hotel. Reasonable rates and a first-class location assured high patronage. Originally called the Lorimer House when built in 1856, its name was changed to the Wales when Charles Wales purchased it.

This mid-19th century shot of 3rd and Main Streets looks south, before the advent of electricity. Gas lamps and dirt streets were the norm at that time. The Cooper Building, on the right, had an Illinois Central Railroad ticket office. Across the street, W.H. Peabody operated a wholesale and jobbing business; Robinson's Crockery was next door; and Poole and Gilliam sold groceries. On the south corner, the Waples House (the sixth building on the left) was built in 1844. The year is about 1858.

In 1858, the Baylies' Commercial College and Telegraphics Institute opened. The name was later changed to Bayless Business College.

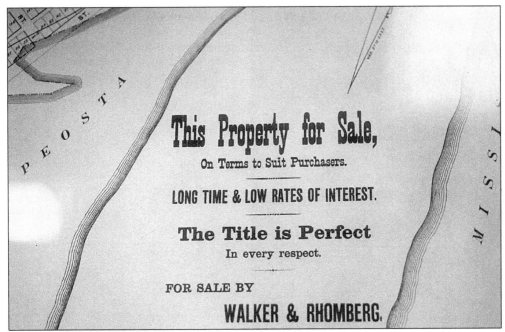

This Property for Sale,

On Terms to Suit Purchasers.

LONG TIME & LOW RATES OF INTEREST.

The Title is Perfect

In every respect.

FOR SALE BY

WALKER & RHOMBERG.

It would be interesting to know for how much money acres were sold on the land separating Peosta Lake and the Mississippi River. The low rates of interest would be inviting as well.

The Illinois Central Railroad crossed the Mississippi by barge until a bridge was built. Number 96 was built in 1857, and operated on the Dubuque and Pacific Railroad.

This is a unique piece of advertising in the mid-19th century. The man appears to have been painted "pleased" with his genuine Alexandre Kid Gloves.

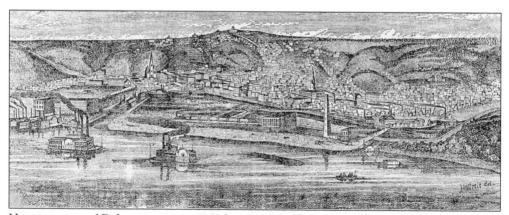

Here is a view of Dubuque prior to 1858 by engraver H.A. Pettit. Note the shot tower in the lower right center.

The custom house was built in 1858 when Dubuque became a port-of-entry on the Mississippi River. This photo dates to about two years later.

1861: Civil War! The Governor's Greys, named to honor the governors of Iowa, organized in April, 1859. Samuel Kirkwood, governor in 1861, pledged the Greys's services to President James Buchanan, making the Iowa unit the first in the nation to tender their services to their country.

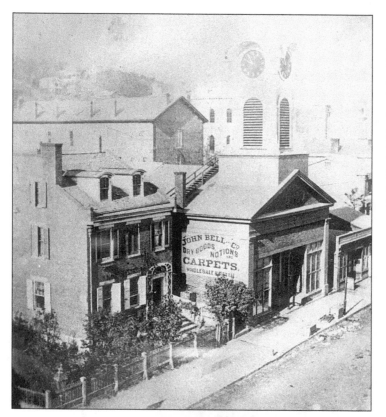

Dubuque was given a perpetual lease by Mr. and Mrs. George Woods to house the town clock in this building, which they owned. John Bell also operated his store here in 1864. At times, the clock was said to be the most accurate town clock in the United States.

On May 25, 1872, cracks were noticed forming in the John Bell Co. building, which fell seconds later, demolishing the store. Two women and a child inside were killed.

The unfamiliar scene in the above photo is the corner of 8th and Main Streets. Known as the Sanford Block, built in the early 1850s, it is shown here in the later 1860s.

This is the home of F.E. Goodrich, greatly enlarged from a Dubuque poster. The border is made up of similar residences.

In the 1860s, Julien Avenue was a good street in dry weather, but a quagmire in rainy times and in the winter. Julien curves to the right (left center), and Hill Street curves to the left, in front of the Diamond House.

Here is the intersection of Bluff (crosswise) and 5th Streets. This picture dates to before 1867. The two grain elevators on the Illinois bank belonged to the Diamond Jo Steamboat Line.

This is Eagle Point, where boats stopped to refuel with firewood. The road in the center of the photo leads to McKnight's Springs.

This photo looks south along the road to McKnight's Springs. The Mississippi is on the left.

The Iowa House Furnishings company is shown here in 1869, on the corner of 10th and Main Streets. The trolley tracks are for horse-drawn cars, which came into existence in 1867. Only St. Louis, Missouri, had streetcars earlier.

The home on the corner of 12th and Iowa Streets was the residence of F.W.H. Sheffield, president of the Merchants National Bank. It was later occupied by George L. Torbert. The row houses in the background make up the Bissell Block. Frederick R. Bissell built the houses on land purchased in the late 1860s.

In the upper photo, the sun is rising on a deserted Main Street at 6:30 a.m., south of the new town clock. The serene pastoral scene below apparently so pleased the man in the photo, that he lay down to enjoy nature for a while.

The police department's patrol wagon is shown here in the mid-19th century. The dappled team appears ready to go at a second's notice.

Two

1869–1886

The Little Maquoketa River, north of Dubuque and south of Sageville, furnished the power for Thompson's Mill to grind grain into flour. It was built in 1852.

Here is a view of Main and 17th Streets, with Madison Street curving up the hill. The wooden steps made it easier to get to the neighborhood on top of the hill.

Connolly's Carriage Manufactory was located on the southwest corner of Iowa and 7th Streets. In this 1880s photo, two different models of the company's broughams are on display. The one on the right could be a four-passenger unit. An elegant way to travel.

24

This is 9th Street approaching Main Street from the west. The frame building was the former Cox residence, while the pillared building was home to the Leven family. This picture was taken about 1869.

Here we see the Cox residence, now the City Hat Factory, and the Millinery & Straw Goods Co. A sewing machine outlet stands between the former building and the customhouse. Across Bluff Street is the "old church." Things have changed since this photo was taken around 1880.

It seems that electricity is still not available as evidenced by the lack of streetcars and lights on Main Street in this photo. A lack of horse-drawn cars dates this image prior to 1867.

The Books & Store's advertisement in the *DuBuque Gazetteer* shows an amazed man crying "Prodigious!" Considering the stock (from pianos to wallpaper), the customer is right.

KEY CITY HOUSE,

Corner Main and Third Sts.,

DUBUQUE, IOWA.

The Key City House, situated on the corner of Main and Third Streets, housed not only travelers and "drummers" but a surgeon and a vinegar brewery as well.

This house on its ledge is addressed on 5th Street. The photo was taken from across the valley.

By 1870, railroads were an up-and-coming phenomenon. In time, these two railroads were combined and renamed. The Chicago, Clinton, Dubuque, and Minnesota was purchased by the Chicago, Milwaukee, and St. Paul in 1880.

The Dubuque Telephone Exchange Company's first directory (consisting of one page), for June 1, 1880, is pictured here.

Several adults and a little girl gather at a picket fence on a bluff overlooking the Mississippi River. East Dubuque is in the background, beyond the island and across the river. In 1877, J.K. Graves, local banker and entrepreneur, started the Hill Street and West Dubuque Railway Company. Small, enclosed steam engines like the one pictured were used, but the idea failed and the equipment was sold to a Florida firm.

J.K. Graves built the Fourth Street Elevator (or Fenelon Place Elevator) in 1882.

This advertising gem for the Fenelon Place Elevator made no phony claims. The view is spectacular.

A cow nonchalantly stands on her own reflection while taking a drink. The building on the left, with the horse-drawn vehicle in front, is Columbia College. This photo dates to approximately 1884.

This photo, taken around 1889, looks west from Locust Street with Washington Park on the left. After three hundred trees were planted, the park was enclosed with a fence to keep wandering livestock out, but people could use the convenient gates.

Here is a view of Eighth and Locust Streets looking north. On the right hand corner across Eighth Street, Connolly's Wagon Shop did business. Across Locust, Oliver Cragin's marble yard offered headstones and other items. This photo also dates to around 1889.

While a hound dog mugs for the cameraman at 9th and Iowa Streets, the latter records the scene. On the extreme left is the H.L. Stout house. William Lawther lived next door, and John Bell, the merchant, lived next to the Lawthers. At the far end of Iowa Street, the German Theological School of the Northwest can be seen. The year is 1889.

A gentleman's calling card from the 1880s is shown here.

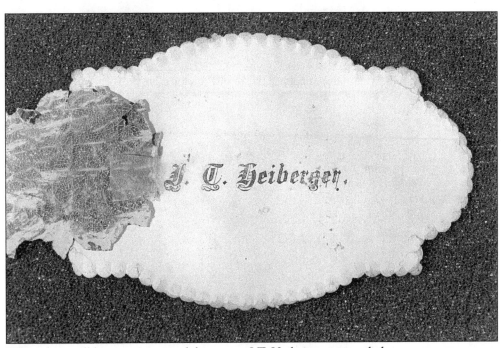

When the small bouquet is opened, his name, J.T. Heiberger, is revealed.

This is an unopened calling card.

This lady's calling card (her name is behind the scroll) is a bit more provocative.

Another unopened lady's calling card is more reserved.

J. O'Connor was known for his sense of humor, especially in advertising his business.

The 11th Street Elevator opened in 1887, serving people who lived in an area known as Quality Hill, where many mansions had been built.

The Second
National
Bank was
located on
the southeast
corner of 6th
and Main
Streets. In
time it would
become
a cafeteria.

The William Marshall foundry and factory produced quality steam boilers of every type.

Three

1886–1901

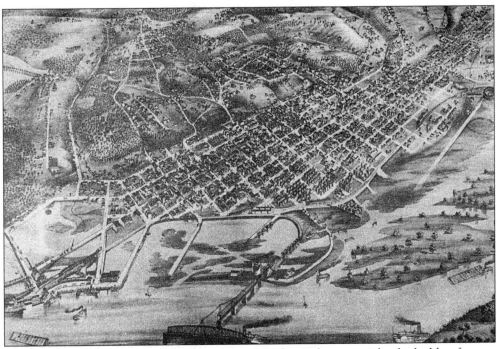

This is an engraving of what the artist thought Dubuque might look like from a bird's perspective.

Dubuque has always been a strong labor union city, as evidenced by the Cabinet Maker's Association.

This shows De Sales Heights in the 1880s. The school became Visitation Academy sometime later. "Ite ad Joseph" (on the shrine at the left of the picture) means "Go to Joseph."

A head-on collision on the Chicago, Milwaukee, & St. Paul Ry killed five people on September 19, 1887.

While the buggies and wagons shown here still park any old way, such will not be the case in time. The trolley cars will be driven by electricity; streets will be well-lighted at night; and more than one inventor is working on a "horseless carriage." This 1890s photo looks north on Main Street from the six hundred block.

A 19th century valentine was elaborately decorated and carried a message of love to the one for whom it was intended.

Here is another valentine from the past. Declarations of love were made in most dramatic ways.

Wartburg Seminary first came to Dubuque in 1853, but the school left because of poor economic conditions. In 1889, the Seminary returned to this building.

By the late 1890s, Dubuque was a thriving city. The huge mansion in the lower center of the photo was called the Redstone, and was a gift of A.A. Cooper (who lived in the huge mansion to the left, across Bluff Street) to his daughter and her husband.

Mrs. Matthews,

→⋇BOARDING⋇HOUSE,⋇←

428 Iowa Street, DUBUQUE, IOWA.

Mrs. Matthews' Boarding House was one of many throughout Dubuque. Her address, 428 Iowa Street, would seem to indicate that she catered to railroad employees, since the house is located less than three blocks from three different railroads.

This picture shows Main Street looking north from the lower end of the six hundred block. Awnings cooled the interior of stores when sun shone on them. The stores on the left side (west) are in shadows and their awnings are up, while those across the street are down, doing their job.

It's not known for certain what the occasion is in this photo. Perhaps the fire department personnel have decorated the wagon for a Memorial Day parade. Or, the casket in the wagon covered with flowers could be a deceased, brother fireman.

A funeral procession stretches from the eight hundred block of Main Street to at least the one thousand block, slowly headed north. Probably no noise other than the clip-clopping of the horses' hooves was heard.

This photo looks west on 8th Avenue from Main Street. The Lincoln Building, with its white marble entrance, housed Baylies' Business College for many years.

The Nonpareil Club held a meeting on Wednesday Eve, October 8, 1890. It was perhaps without equal.

Here is the cover of the invitation used to bring people to the grand opening celebration of the Great Bridge (the Wagon Bridge) that spanned the Mississippi River.

This is the actual invitation to the November 29, 1887 occasion.

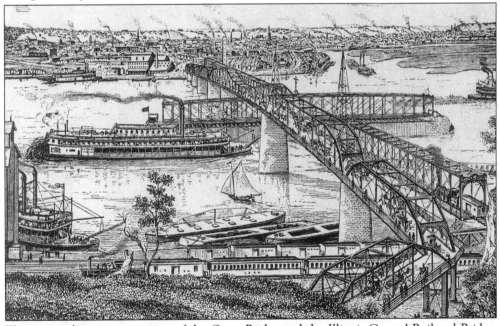

This image shows an engraving of the Great Bridge and the Illinois Central Railroad Bridge, each of which paralleled the other. The engraving was included with the invitation.

Happy 1891 from Manhart, Loes, and Co. They were located at 7th and Clay (Central Avenue) Streets.

A raft of logs arrives in Dubuque, destined for the saw mills.

Nicholas Palen, a local businessman, built a three-story building on the corner of 18th and Couler Streets in 1895, a great year for new buildings.

The building constructed by Nicholas Palen displayed "N. Palen 1895" in the center above the two windows. Notice the fire escape on the right.

Dubuque Central High School was completed in 1895. The building, constructed of redstone, was a beautiful example of Richardsonian Romanesque architecture.

The Levens family moved out of their stately home on the left, and a dentist's office now occupies the center portion. The north wing houses a metal repairing company, and a retail shop is located in the south wing. The Bank and Insurance Building was completed in 1895, and its tenants were in their new offices before Thanksgiving.

The Security Building housed many different types of offices on the upper floors, and shops on the ground floor. Notice the glass canopy on the left, and the one on the Grand Opera House on the right. The building was completed in 1896.

If it really polished furniture and brass so well, and got rid of white marks on table tops caused by alcohol, why did they stop making it? This is a good offer on the special coupon. The establishment was located in the Security Building.

49

BIRDSEYE VIEW OF THE BREWERY, SHOWING BOTTLING AND SHIPPING DEPARTMENTS.

Four of Dubuque's major breweries formed the Dubuque Brewing and Malting companies. The first brew was barreled in 1896. Their leading beer was Banquet Beer. The buildings above housed the entire operation, and hundreds of barrels were shipped out of Dubuque on the Chicago Great Western Railroad, whose tracks and sidings can be seen in the photo.

50

The camera captures Main Street in this photo from the 4th Street intersection. Bartels Theatre was the first such establishment on that corner.

Across Main Street from Bartels Theatre, D.C. Glasser Tobacco Co. did business.

R. Herrmann & Sons

Forty years experience in the Furniture Business

QUALITY GOODS ONLY

DUBUQUE'S
LEADING

House Furnishers

Fine Upholstering
and Finishing

Furniture Made
to Order

1000 MAIN ST.

R. Herrmann & Sons had 40 years of experience in the furniture business. The building, on the corner of 10th and Main Streets, was built in 1894.

Becker–Hazleton imported and wholesaled thousands of pieces of crockery, fine china, and glassware over the years.

The accounting room of the Dubuque Fire and Marine Insurance Company is shown in this photo. Their offices were in the Bank and Insurance Building.

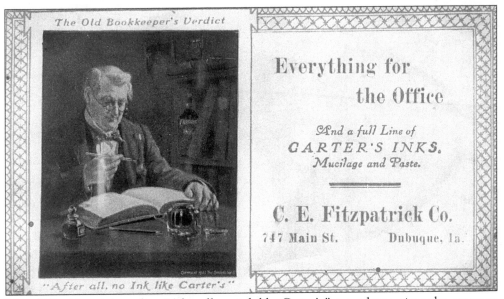

The old bookkeeper's verdict, "After all, no ink like Carter's," proved true, since the company remained in business for years to come.

The Henry Trenkle Company began as a butcher shop in 1894 on 14th Street, and moved to the location above in 1897 to specialize in sausage. His products became known all over the Midwest.

The Julien Hotel is on the northwest corner of Main and 2nd Streets. The Union Electric Company went into business in August, 1900. On the left side of the photo, the man in shirt sleeves and straw sailor hat stands beneath the Key City Natatorium's sign.

The JULIEN

W. C. KEELEY,
Manager.

Dubuque's Leading Hotel

All Modern Improvements

LOCAL and LONG DISTANCE TELEPHONES
· · · IN EVERY ROOM. · · ·

The Julien, Dubuque's leading hotel, offered local and long distance telephone service in every room.

The original Finley Hospital is on the left. It originally housed 40 beds, until the building on the right was completed in 1898. The first building became a nurses' training facility and graduated four registered nurses two years later in 1900. The view above was taken about 1899.

A damp, hazy, rainy day in 1892 holds 8th and Main Streets in its grip at 2:25 p.m. Roshek's Department Store is on the left, and Whiner's place of business is on the right. D & H Red Letter Free Day Stamps are being offered at the corner of the Security Building.

Four

ARCHITECTURE

The simplest of lines and angles make up this Iowa schoolhouse in the 19th century. Schoolhouses dotted the countryside of every state, and it was in such one-room schools that the basic fundamentals were learned from a single teacher. While the teacher (woman or man) taught one grade, older students helped younger ones learn to read, or to "cipher."

The Rhomberg "steamboat-style" house on top of the hill overlooked the city, while Rhomberg employees lived in the two "steamboat-style" houses below. A vineyard lay between the structures. The board fences at the bottom of the picture were for economical privacy, and kept the livestock that the family owned secure.

Central High School in 19th century Dubuque was of Richardsonian Romanesque architecture. The outside façade was redstone.

Built in the latter part of the 1880s and early 1890s, the Illinois Central Railroad depot dominated the southern end of Dubuque. The first floor had ticket offices, a waiting room, a coffee shop, Railway Express Agency offices, and storage areas. The second floor was similar to a hotel, where railroad men could sleep when not working if they didn't live in town.

This is the J.K. Graves home. Its location prompted him to build the Fenelon Place Elevator, which allowed him to reach his bank more quickly. It is a bit eclectic in style, and includes an Italianate tower.

The Richardsonian Romanesque home of Frank Stout (left), a lumber man, displayed seven different types of woodwork to show customers the potential of beautiful woods in a home. The Custer house seems to be a Queen Anne mansion, with a Byzantine-style roof and Richardsonian Romanesque expansiveness. The building on the right is Italianate.

Mathias Ham, one of Dubuque's earliest settlers, commissioned John Francis Rague, a well-known architect, to design and build this Italianate mansion in 1856.

The home on the corner of 15th and Main Streets displays the classic lines of a Second Empire architectural style, with its easily identified Mansard roof.

Sullivanesque architectural styling graced the Bank and Insurance Building, which was built on the corner of 9th and Main Streets. It was completed in 1895.

The Italianate mansion on top of the rocky bluff, and its towered, eclectic neighbor atop the huge retaining wall, share the same wooden staircase. To the left, a four-story home has been built into the side of the bluff, complete with a cottage-style roof.

The simple lines of the German Congregational Church were built of wood in the board and batten method, prior to 1887.

Another view of downtown Dubuque pays attention to the various styles of architecture, from turreted Romanesque mansions, to Second Empire Mansard roofs, to Dutch step gable roofs, cupolas, and Federalist styles.

Mount St. Joseph's style of architecture is Romanesque with an Empire Mansard roof.

The New Melleray Trappist Monks' main building is of Gothic design. Notice the windmill atop a hexagonal tower that furnished well water indoors.

St. Joseph's Sanitarium for the mentally ill was a combination of Romanesque and Gothic architecture. The pointed dormers are Gothic, and the round-topped windows are Romanesque.

The original town clock displays Romanesque features, and combines nicely with the Italian roof line. Note the house on the left and the home on the right. The one on the left has a Dutch-style roof, while the other has a more conventional roof with an overhang.

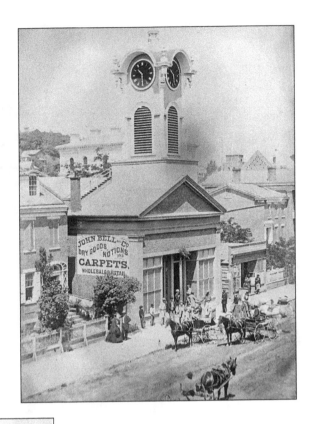

Majestic Theatre

On the evening of November 16, 1910, the initial performance was given at the New Majestic Theater. The opening of this beautiful playhouse proved an innovation to Dubuque theater goers as well as a source of pride to the city and a satisfaction to the owner and manager, Mr. Jake

Rosenthal. The newly built structure stands upon the site of the old Bijou, which was destroyed by fire less than thirteen months ago. The architects and contractors who had the building in charge have produced the most beautiful and safest theater in Iowa at a cost of $90,000. Architecturally, the Majestic is replica of a theater in

Paris, long considered one of the handsomest in the French capital. According to the statement of experts who have examined the building, it is as fire-proof in every respect as possible. The Majestic Theater is affiliated with the Keith and Proctor circuits in the east and the Orpheum and the Kohl and Castle circuits in the

west ,and as these cover the entire Advanced Vaudeville field from New York to San Francisco, the management has first and exclusive call on the services of all leading stars and specialties. Patrons may therefore be assured that they will enjoy the best of attractions in the world of varieties.

The Majestic Theatre was built on the site of the old Bijou, which in turn followed the first theatre on the corner of 4th and Main Streets. Architecturally, the Majestic is a replica of a theatre in Paris, France.

This view of downtown Dubuque from atop 5th Street shows more styles of architecture than can be included in the caption.

F.W. Woodward's home on Wartburg Place displays an Italianate tower, along with intricate cast iron pillars and décor.

De Sales Heights changed its name to Academy of the Visitation, as evidenced by the sign above the main entrance. It was built with Dutch style roofing.

Thomas J. Connolly's residence on the northern edge of Jackson Park (Iowa Street is on the right) was a good example of Richardsonian Romanesque. The double Byzantine towers in the right center of the photograph are part of the German Theological Seminary. Across Iowa Street is an example of Empire architecture with a Mansard roof.

Different styles of architecture were displayed on Main Street in this view looking south from 5th Street.

St. Raphael's Cathedral, of Gothic architecture, dominates most any view of the neighborhood in which it was built. Father Samuel Mazzuchelli was the original architect of St. Raphael's, and of dozens of other churches in the area. Note the high, wooden fences used to restrain livestock.

The Custom House.

Looking Down River.

Romanesque architecture dominated the multi-chimneyed customhouse. Various styles are evident in the lower photo.

The Richardson home (left) was an excellent example of Stick architecture, a rare style in Dubuque.

The main building of the new Dubuque German College and Seminary utilized several types of architecture to produce an eclectic style.

St. Mary's Casino on White Street used an abundance of Romanesque architecture. The building contained a gymnasium and smaller meeting rooms on the lower level and second floor.

Five

INDUSTRY

With two riding plows, the four-horse teams will finish the field before sundown. Note the fly nets on the animals' backs and sides to protect them from bites.

Large families assured that the work would be done on a 19th century farm. Here, an unidentified family poses for a traveling photographer, with their three teams of horses.

Photographers traveled the countryside making part of their living by recording family histories through photographs. We'll never know why the man on the steps preferred not to join the family and be seen more clearly.

As if posing for a Currier and Ives engraving, this obviously successful farm family had no qualms about posing for the photographer. Could the cart on the left have been made by A.A. Cooper's Wagon Factory in Dubuque?

What appears to be a barn raising was occasion to make a photographic record. Even the five women, who probably cooked for the 50 plus men building the structure, were asked to be in the picture.

Two views of an Iowa farm house are seen here. Such homes seldom grace the countryside anymore. Still, the occasion prompted the family to dress up in their finest.

Here, the same house is shown from a different angle. The windmill, not visible in the other photo, is working to bring fresh well water up to the livestock tank. The farm dog is clearly seen in this shot. The house is a saltbox style

An unusual sight in the 19th century was an abandoned homestead. Notice the opening for an outside fire, probably used for cooking during the hot summers.

The three men in the wagon on the right are ready to continue picking up potatoes after the six-horse-drawn potato picker passes. Notice the full-grown potatoes on the ground.

The monks at the New Melleray Trappist Monastery are moving their well-maintained Deering binder. It would take a three-horse team to use the implement in the fields.

The first-floor windows of City Hall (across the street on the left) were 11 feet high. The limestone sills were the height of a wagon bed, to make it easier to unload produce for the Farmers' Market. The market began in 1858, and grew to eventually cover 16 city blocks after City Hall reclaimed the first floor.

Here are three checks drawn on the First National Bank of Dubuque in 1868. The middle check was signed by Platt Smith, an attorney and entrepreneur who was a railroad power and developed transportation in the 1860s and 1870s.

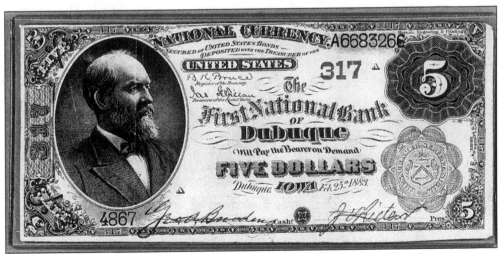

This five dollar bill was issued by the First National Bank of Dubuque in 1883. It was common practice for banks in the 19th century to issue their own currency when necessary.

77

Part of the Dubuque Lumber and Coal Company's fleet of horse-drawn wagons is shown here.

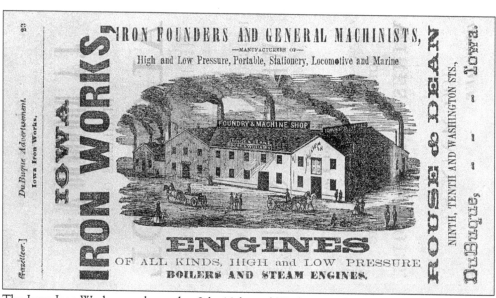

The Iowa Iron Works were located at 9th, 10th, and Washington Streets, where they produced various steam engines.

Gun Powder Manufactory—Carriage Manufactory—Drug Store.

LAFLINS' POWDER CO.,

MANUFACTURERS OF

GUN POWDER

AND DEALERS IN

POWDER, SHOT, SAFETY FUSE. &C.

AGENTS FOR THE ST. LOUIS SHOT TOWER COMP'Y.

Office, No. 56 Main Street,

DUBUQUE, - - - - - - - IOWA.

LAFLINS & SMITH.   J. M. BOIES.   J. TURCK.   S. TURCK.

THOS. CONNOLLEY,

MANUFACTURER AND DEALER IN

CARRIAGES,

WAGONS,

SLEIGHS.

ETC., ETC.

Corner of Locust and Eighth Sts.,

DUBUQUE, IOWA.

All work made of the best Eastern material, and warranted to give perfect satisfaction. Particular attention given to light work.

The ad on top for Laflins' Powder Co. states that the company acted as agents for the St. Louis Shot Tower Company. Laflin was located at 56 Main Street in Dubuque. The ad below tells of Thomas Connolly's Manufactory, where carriages, wagons, and sleighs were produced.

Titus Schmid & Co.,

PROPRIETORS OF

IOWA BREWERY,

MANUFACTURERS OF

LAGER BEER.

DUBUQUE, - IOWA.

The Iowa Brewery and the Western Brewery both manufactured lager beer. But so did Glab's Northern, Heeb's Brewery, Peaslee's Brewery, and the Dubuque Brewery and Malting Co., which combined most of the other breweries in Dubuque, except for Rhomberg's Dubuque Star Brewery.

Tschirgi & Schwind,

PROPRIETORS OF

WESTERN BREWERY

MANUFACTURERS OF

Lager Beer,

The office for the Standard Lumber Company, Dubuque's largest, began business in 1880.

The Shot Tower was purchased by a St. Louis firm that prevented it from producing shot. The Standard Lumber Company later used it as a watch tower to look out for any fires that might start.

Here, the Wagon Bridge is in the process of being constructed parallel to the Illinois Central Railroad Bridge. It was completed and opened in November, 1897.

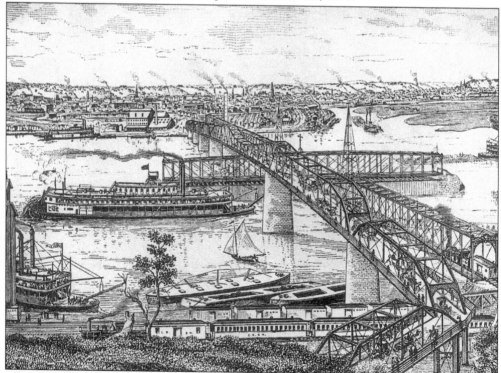

This engraved picture of the new bridge accompanied the invitation to the grand opening of the Wagon Bridge.

A log raft is shown here being pushed down the river by the *Juniata*. Notice the heavy hawsers extending from the corners of the raft to a little beyond mid-boat on the sternwheeler. The ropes helped direct the raft.

This is winter time in the Chicago, Milwaukee, & St. Paul Ry yards. The buildings from the center of the photo to the left were car shops. At one time, the Milwaukee employed 2,200 people in Dubuque.

A Union Electric Company employee has lowered the lamp at the intersection of 32nd Street and Couler Avenue. The Heim Hotel is the building to the right, and the structure behind it is part of the Heim Brickyard.

Shown from a different angle, the Dubuque Malt and Brewery Company's building at 30th Street and Jackson Boulevard is an impressive sight.

John Ellwanger, a prominent Dubuque liquor merchant, served as an executive in other Key City businesses. The above building at 398 Main Street housed his store.

The Dubuque Mattress Factory was established in 1876 and incorporated in February, 1884, by John Kapp and Henry Sauer.

The Eagle Point Bridge that entered Wisconsin was one of the last privately-owned toll bridges to span the Mississippi. The company, organized in 1894, was headed by Joseph A. Rhomberg.

Six

TRANSPORTATION

For more than a few years, horses were the main power for transportation, only to be replaced by the steamboat, and then the steam locomotive in the 19th century.

Four men pose with the load of Prairie Queen Flour they've just unloaded from the narrow gauge boxcar, which was shipped in from Dubuque via Bellevue. The man standing is the stationmaster.

Teams of mules, as well as horses, were used to haul produce to and from farms, towns, railroads, and factories.

The G. *Boner* pushes its raft of
logs south on the Mississippi.
Note the rowboats on the left,
sitting on the raft itself.

Rock Cut on I. C. R. R. South of Dubuque.

An Illinois Central Railroad engine works hard, pulling its train up from the Mississippi River
Valley. Heading west, it will pass through Rockdale and then Center Grove, Iowa, before
arriving in Peosta, Epworth, and Farley.

The Rockdale, Iowa mill, which was serviced by the Illinois Central Railroad, was just south and west of Dubuque.

Center Grove, Iowa, just west of Dubuque, was a thriving little community. The Illinois Central Railroad, successor to the Dubuque and Sioux City Railroad, served the area.

A sternwheeler puts in at the Diamond Jo facilities to take on a load of wood. The Diamond Jo Lines was one of the largest companies on the Upper Mississippi.

Frentress Lake, south of East Dubuque, Illinois, was a great place for fishing, swimming, and boating.

When the Mississippi froze, boats would hurry to a harbor such as Dubuque's Ice Harbor and remain there for the cold months.

The Inspector's Certificate for the steamship *Minnesota*, which expired on April 11, 1871, is shown here.

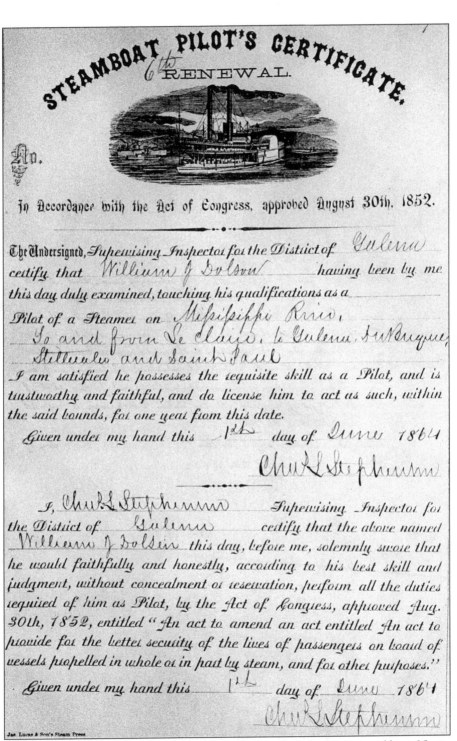

STEAMBOAT PILOT'S CERTIFICATE.
6th RENEWAL.

No.

In Accordance with the Act of Congress, approved August 30th, 1852.

The Undersigned, Supervising Inspector for the District of _Galena_ certify that _William J Dolson_ having been by me this day duly examined, touching his qualifications as a Pilot of a Steamer on _Mississippi River,_ _To and from Le Claire, to Galena, Dubuque,_ _Stillwater and Saint Paul_ I am satisfied he possesses the requisite skill as a Pilot, and is trustworthy and faithful, and do license him to act as such, within the said bounds, for one year from this date.

Given under my hand this _1st_ day of _June_ 1864

Chs L Stephenson

I, _Chs L Stephenson_ Supervising Inspector for the District of _Galena_ certify that the above named _William J Dolson_ this day, before me, solemnly swore that he would faithfully and honestly, according to his best skill and judgment, without concealment or reservation, perform all the duties required of him as Pilot, by the Act of Congress, approved Aug. 30th, 1852, entitled "An act to amend an act entitled An act to provide for the better security of the lives of passengers on board of vessels propelled in whole or in part by steam, and for other purposes."

Given under my hand this _1st_ day of _June_ 1864

Chs L Stephenson

Jas Lucas & Son's Steam Press

A Steamboat Pilot's Certificate (6th renewal) for William J. Dolson is pictured here. Notice the old English spelling of Mississippi. The certificate is dated June 1, 1864.

93

Rail traffic improved immensely once Andrew Carnegie's iron bridge was completed in 1868.

Here is a view of Carnegie's bridge with the swing section open for river traffic. The tracks entered a sharply-curved tunnel in the bluff, and swung to the right to enter East Dubuque, Illinois.

J.K. Graves promoted the idea for the Hill Street and West Dubuque Steam Railway in 1877. In 1884, the H.S. & W.D. Steam Ry pulled up its tracks.

Horse-drawn cars worked better, as long as floods didn't get too deep, as shown here in the 1880s.

When electricity was developed to power streetcars through an overhead trolley, reliable public transportation was achieved.

State-of-the-art trolley cars pose at the corner of 8th and Main Streets, five minutes before noon. At 12:00, whistles from several different factories will sound the noon hour lunch break.

Other than mechanized means of transportation and horse-powered devices, steps were also used to conquer the hills of Dubuque. Here, the second of at least three stairways is shown, going to the continuation of Main Street on top of the bluff.

These are the steps used by J.K. Graves to walk to Fenelon Place and enter his elevator railway to go downtown to his office. Graves' home is in the background.

Elevators proved successful in Dubuque. Ten years after installing a one-car elevator, J.K. Graves had it rebuilt as a two-car, inclined railway as shown here in 1893.

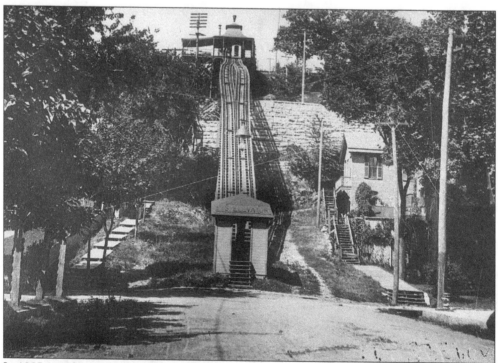

In 1887, another inclined railway was begun. A two-grade track was laid until the retaining wall could be finished. This elevator was on 11th Street.

The track work was leveled to one grade once the retaining wall was completed. The last step was to form an arch over the tracks.

In need of repairs in 1898, the Illinois Central Railroad Bridge was rebuilt, but back in service by 1900. Above, a switch engine pushes a cut of cars to Illinois. To the right is part of the Dubuque Star Brewery. To the left is the Shot Tower, which was used as a fire watch tower for the Standard Lumber Company.

This is a western view, looking at Dubuque over the Wagon Bridge and railroad bridge. Notice that the second span (the highest) on the Wagon Bridge is a suspension span.

The Wisherd Line's *Geo. Hill* stops in Dubuque for fuel, and loading and unloading.

North Western Line's *War Eagle*, a side-wheeler, appears to be loading or unloading cargo. Notice the carriage supervisor watching the proceedings.

TORPEDO BOAT ERICSSON IN CONSTRUCTION BY THE IOWA IRON WORKS.

The torpedo boat *Ericsson* is shown here under construction at the Iowa Iron Works.

The torpedo boat *Ericsson* leaves Dubuque's Ice Harbor, where it was built by the Iowa Iron Works. Its destination is Washington. It is in the tow of the steamboat *J.S. Streator*.

The steamer *W.W.* is here about to pass beneath the Wagon Bridge heading north on the Mississippi. It appears that the *W.W.* is an excursion boat. The warehouses in the background are where the riverboats are loaded, and are located in East Dubuque.

Here is the Diamond Jo steamer *St. Paul* at Eagle Point dock in Dubuque. Such boats were built to last a long time, providing the boiler didn't explode.

Before the advent of bridges, freight cars were ferried across the Mississippi by ferry boats such as the *Campbell*. Note the locomotive loading a Chicago, Burlington, and Quincy boxcar aboard.

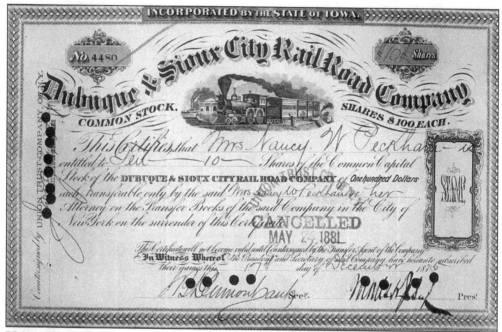

This is a photo of ten shares of common stock issued to Mrs. Nancy W. Peckham in December, 1875. In time, the Illinois Central, through the efforts of Edward H. Harriman, bought the Dubuque and Sioux City Railroad.

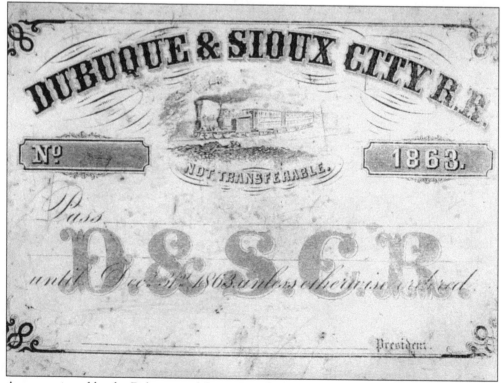

A pass, as issued by the Dubuque and Sioux City Railroad, is shown here.

DuBuque and Sioux City,

AND

BUBUQUE SOUTHWESTERN RAILWAYS.

(FOR DISTANCES SEE PAGE 687)

CONNECTIONS.

Connects at DuBuque with the East and South, by the Illinois Central Railway.

The BuBuque and Sioux City Railway connects at Farley Junction with the DuBuque South Western Railway to Marion; thence by Stage (6 miles) to Cedar Rapids, connecting there the same evening with the train going East for Mount Vernon, Lisbon, Mechanicsville, DeWitt, Camanche, Lyons, and Clinton; also at Cedar Rapids, by train the next morning for Toledo, Marshalltown, Nevada, Boonsboro and Des Moines.

Stages leave Cedar Rapids every morning for Iowa City, returning to Cedar Rapids every evening, connecting, after the arrival of the train from the West, by Stage to Marion the same evening.

Stage from Farley to Cascade on Mondays, Thursdays, and Saturdays.

Stages from Dyersville for Colesburg and Elkader on Mondays, Wednesdays, and Fridays.

Stage connections at Earlville on Mondays, Wednesdays, and Fridays, for Strawberry Point, West Union, Fayette, etc.

Stage daily from Delaware to Delhi.

Stage connections at Manchester on Tuesdays, Thursdays, and Saturdays, for Strawberry Point, West Union, Fayette, etc.

Stage daily from Winthrop for Quasqueton.

This shows the Dubuque and Sioux City Ry and its connections with other railroads and stagecoaches.

Here, a trolley car trundles into Dubuque along Sageville Road. To the right is Nutwood (racing) Park. The line also extended to Stewart's Park.

105

The Chicago, Burlington, and Northern Railroad's depot (shown above) became the Chicago, Burlington, and Quincy Railroad through a series of mergers.

The clean, simple lines of the Chicago Great Western Railway make it an attractive building. Offices were on the second floor, while the waiting room, a ticket agent, and the baggage room occupied the first floor.

An open-platform passenger coach pulls out of Dubuque's Milwaukee Road station, heading north behind its train.

No matter how good business was, it usually ground to a halt in the event of an accident, as shown by this head-on collision of 1887 in which five people died.

Pulpit Rock (on the right) witnesses trains passing east and west daily. The Dubuque and Sioux City line was eventually bought by the Illinois Central Railroad.

Here are steamboats rafting logs downriver, probably to Clinton, Iowa, past the Key City of Dubuque.

The original trestle bridge that spanned the mouth of Catfish Creek was built by the Dubuque and Bellevue Railroad. In the scene above, it is owned by the Chicago, Milwaukee, and St. Paul Ry.

J. Rhomberg signed passes for his transit line.

Going to Shawondassee was always fun. One could fish off the government wing dam, swim, play ball, and picnic.

While the railroads stole business from steamboat lines, trolley cars continued to carry people around Dubuque. Still, there were (and would be for some time) people who continued to believe in old dobbin and a wagon or buggy.

Seven

ENTERTAINMENT

Swiss Valley Park, near Dubuque, became a much loved picnic area in the late 19th century, for people as well as for the above herd of white-tail deer.

Shawondassee, a private resort area south of Dubuque on the Mississippi River, could be reached by horse and buggy over the road, by boat, or by the Chicago, Milwaukee, and St. Paul Ry, whose tracks hugged the western bank of the river.

The Italianate home of H. Stout was the beginning of the Y.M.C.A. The auditorium next to it had plenty of room for exercising, volleyball, and other indoor sports.

The Dubuque Shooting Society is one of the oldest clubs extant in Dubuque. Founded in 1856, they moved to their new location along Sageville Road in 1887. The original name was "Dubuque Schuetzen Gesellschaft."

The Dubuque Shooting Society fired on a 160-yard range at 30th Street and Jackson Boulevard. When the Dubuque and Northwestern Railroad's track cut across the firing range, a new home was needed and eventually found north of the city, west of Sageville Road.

The Grand—Dubuque's leading Opera House—was built between 1889 and 1890. It featured a seating capacity of 1,100, and a large stage 42 feet deep. Eager crowds of "first-nighters" paid $5 each to enjoy Georges Bizet's opera *Carmen*.

Baseball, the great American pastime, was always popular in Dubuque in the decades after 1855, when it was first played in the Key City. In 1879, the Dubuque team defeated the two top National League teams, claiming the world championship. In 1895, the team moved into the park above, between 24th and 25th Streets and Jackson Boulevard.

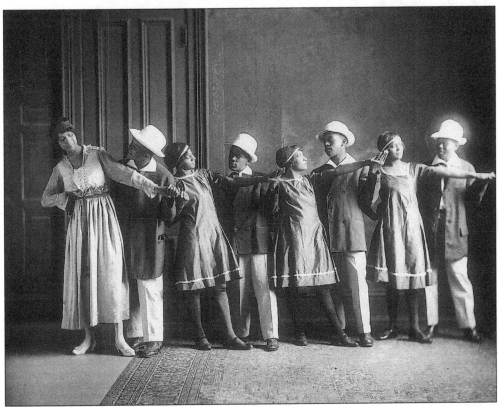

A local show troupe strikes a pose that appeared in one of their productions. The four men are dressed in similar costumes, while three of the four women are dressed alike. Why the one on the left is in different garb will probably remain forever a mystery.

It's summertime, and the circus train pulled into Dubuque before dawn. At midday, it's time for the parade to whet people's appetites for the big show. Indian elephants plod along on their own shadows, followed by the first of several Bactrian camels.

While the circus parade continues north on Locust Street, the passing of a lion cage wagon probably increased the heartbeats of the umbrella-protected viewers.

The Imperial Orchestra of Dubuque poses on stage, with instruments at the ready, waiting to break into another piece of music. The sax man and pianist are out of uniform with their dark shoes.

According to its advertising, the Wales Hotel was close to downtown stores, shops, theatres, and most forms of entertainment. It was located on the corner of 9th and Bluff Streets.

While Dubuque has been known for heavy snowstorms for years, the above photo, taken in front of Central High School on 15th and Locust Streets, shows just enough snow for the people to enjoy a ride in a one-horse open sleigh.

Henry L. Stout owned Nutwood, a 1,150-pound trotting stallion, for which Nutwood Park—a race track—was named. After paying $22,000 for the horse, Stout's "folly" had earned $650,000 when the animal died in 1896.

Highland Stock Farm, home of Nutwood, had its own race course for the champion trotter to work out.

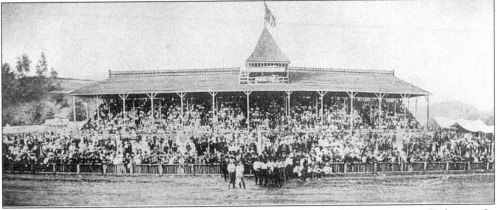

Nutwood Park, located east of Sageville Road, was the home of horse racing in Dubuque. In time, the track became so popular that excursion trains arrived from across the United States. Later, boxing matches were offered at night, and riverboat trips were available as well.

William G. Stewart contributed much to Dubuque, but most of his contributions are forgotten when compared to his gift of several acres to the city in 1890. His main hope was the development of a park where families could picnic and commune with nature. In 1891, the Allen and Swiney Motor Line Company purchased an additional 40 acres. In 1900, it was renamed Union Park.

Eight

DUBUQUERS

Kids have not changed in centuries, as runners, skis, ice skates, and anything else that would slide on snow (as proved by the 1890s photo above) thrilled them.

Four little girls play a game at Stewart Park, letting go of some of the pent-up city steam. Notice the hitching post above the girl's head on the left.

Even in the late 19th century, the fall of the year brought out the urge in boys to play some form of football.

A family gathers in the backyard to forever record visiting relatives. While it should have been a time to smile, everyone seems rather sober—especially the little girl in the hammock, who appears sad.

It was usually an uncommon event to have a four-generation picture taken in the 19th century. From left to right are great-grandmother, grandmother (seated, holding the fourth generation), and mother.

This is the wedding picture of Mr. and Mrs. Anthony Pfohl. Two sons, Anthony C. Pfohl, M.D., and architect Louis Pfohl, became rather well-known in Dubuque, and one of them in New York City as well.

Andrew Young McDonald came to Dubuque in 1856, two years after arriving in the United States. He founded the A.Y. McDonald Manufacturing Company, which produced pumps and plumbing supplies. He was a member of the Governors's Greys during the Civil War.

Republican William Boyd Allison was elected to the Senate in 1872 after serving as a congressman. He lost his bid for the Republican nomination to William McKinley, who won the presidency in 1896.

David Brenner Henderson was a Scot by birth, but a Dubuquer by choice. He was the first elected person from west of the Mississippi to achieve the position of Speaker of the House of Representatives. This was the highest office he could attain, having been born in Scotland.

A young lady models the chic attire of the very late 19th century.

This is a family picture showing the Bernhardt Tigges family. Bernhardt (with a white beard) was born in 1797, and died in 1890. His wife, Agnes, was born in 1813. Their five children prospered, and Bernhardt and Agnes celebrated their 50th wedding anniversary in 1889.

A bunch of boys were whooping it up in a tree, playing guitars and singing the hit songs of the day.

An attractive little girl strikes a pose for the photographer, with gloves and a house cap.

Throughout this book, high fences have been referred to as keeping livestock inside. While only one chicken is visible, the fence also retained the dogs, but not the children.

This is the graduating class of 1900 from Central High School. Notice that most of the graduates are looking off to the photographer's left, while only two look to the right, and six young ladies peer directly into the lens.